Animals in the Wild

Parrot

by Vincent Serventy

STECK-VAUGHN
C O M P A N Y

There are more than 300 kinds of parrots in the
world. Most have bright, colorful feathers.
This blue and yellow macaw is from South America.

Parrots can use their feet like hands. This scarlet macaw is holding a twig. Parrots have strong beaks for cracking open seeds.

The peach-faced lovebird is from Africa. It is
smaller than the macaw and makes a good pet.

The parrot in *Treasure Island* may have been
an African grey. They learn to talk easily.

Rose-ringed parakeets live in rural areas and in cities in northern Africa and India. This one has made its nest in a hole in an old wall.

The kea is a New Zealand parrot. It lives in the mountains. Keas eat garbage and sometimes steal food from campers and picnickers.

Australia has been called the land of parrots.
This palm cockatoo measures two feet long. It
is the largest of the Australian parrots.

The beautiful pink cockatoo lives in the drier parts of Australia. Like many other wild parrots, it eats seeds, nuts, and fruits.

The sulphur-crested cockatoo has a loud, harsh call. It is a popular pet and can mimic human

voices and animal sounds. It lives in the
forests of northern and eastern Australia.

The native people of Australia expected rain when they saw flocks of red-tailed black cockatoos flying in the sky.

These little corellas are coming in to land.
When corellas fly in huge flocks, they look
like clouds in the Australian sky.

This beautiful pink and grey galah is also
known as a rose-breasted cockatoo. Galahs
can be found over most of the Australian
mainland and even in city suburbs.

Cockatiels were once called cockatoo parrots.
Like most cockatoos, the cockatiel has a
crest, a tuft of showy feathers on its head.
And like the parrot, it has a long tail.

The crimson rosella is one of the most colorful
of the rosellas. It lives in the forests of
eastern Australia. When snow falls in the

mountains, the rosellas fly to the lowlands
for the winter. This pair of crimson rosellas
is searching for seeds beneath the snow.

These budgerigars, also known as budgies, are
drinking at a water hole. Like most parrots,
budgies eat seeds, and drink water every day.

Here, flocks of budgerigars perch on dead trees. From a distance, the budgies look like leaves, making the trees seem alive.

The small ground parrot makes its nest in
grass clumps and finds its food on the ground.
Most parrots build nests in holes in trees.
All parrots' eggs are white.

The lorikeet has a tongue with a tip like a brush. It uses its tongue to lap up sweet nectar from flowers. This musk lorikeet lives in southeastern Australia.

The beautiful rainbow lorikeet lives in the
forests of northern and eastern Australia.
Lorikeets often fly to city gardens to search
for nectar from flowering shrubs and trees.

Bird lovers in Australia often put out
honey for rainbow lorikeets. In this bird
sanctuary, wild lorikeets perch on a girl's
head. Others wait their turn for some honey.

First Steck-Vaughn Edition 1992

First published in the United States 1986
by Raintree Publishers , A Division of Steck-Vaughn Company.

First published in Australia in 1985 by
John Ferguson Pty. Ltd.
100 Kippax Street
Surry Hills, NSW 2010

The North American hardcover edition published by arrangement
with Gareth Stevens Inc.

Acknowledgments are due to Vincent Serventy for all photographs in
this book except the following:
Donald and Molly Trounson: front cover, p. 8, p. 14; J.L.G. Grande, Bruce
Coleman Ltd: p. 3, back cover; Hans Reinhard, Bruce Coleman Ltd: p. 4;
Jane Burton, Bruce Coleman Ltd: p. 5; M.F. Soper, Bruce Coleman Ltd: p.
7; Dave Watts: p. 20.

Library of Congress number: 86-17793

Library of Congress Cataloging in Publication Data

Serventy, Vincent.
  Parrot.

  (Animals in the wild)
  Summary: Portrays various kinds of parrots in their natural environments.
  1. Parrots—Juvenile literature. [1. Parrots]
I. Title. II. Series.
QL696.P7S47 1986   598'.71   86-17793

ISBN 0-8172-2705-9   hardcover library binding

ISBN 0-8114-6885-2   softcover binding

  3 4 5 6 7 8 9   95 94